CW00459481

KERATOCONUS AND ME

Beth + Tony

Best Wishes

Ash

Ashley Winter

For more information please follow Ash on Twitter @Ash_Adventure

WE KERATOCONICS STRUGGLE READING BOOKS FOR LONG PERIODS OF TIME, SO THIS BOOK HAS BEEN KEPT SHORT AND SWEET WITH BIGGER FONT TO HELP THOSE LIKE ME.

Attending one of many appointments.

FOR MY FAMILY

"I'm not blind by any stretch of the imagination; however I struggle with my eyesight and varying other issues linked to Keratoconus causing problems in many aspects of life"

Ash Winter

KERATOCONUS AND ME

A personal account of the struggle with Keratoconus, from an arctic expedition to alpine ski racing, pushing Keratoconus to its limits!

DIAGNOSIS

Growing up I never thought I would join the forces, however the way our family carried on it wasn't a surprise to find out that over half of us cousins has been in the Army one way or another, looking back to bonfire night aged about 14 we had a family get together as we often did, the adults would have a great catch up as we would dress as soldiers from many different decades, miss matched uniforms, stick guns, pine cone grenades and usually a beret of some kind stolen from our fathers.

Rockets lighting up the sky, the bangs sounding like gunfire we all thought this was the closest thing we could get to the real thing, lying on a grass verge taking cover from the explosions and gunfire on my right a cousin who joined the TA and on my left my brother who for some reason joined the infantry, maybe it was this particular night that excited him to join up?

Super-cousins at Nan's.

Back in the house belonging to my grandparents, then to be our house and now my brothers family were the grown-ups, did they know that this night along with many other similar get together would have such an impact on all of our lives, we usually gave ourselves an objective of some sort and other times we would split into goodies and baddies, on this particular poignant night we had the objective of securing "the green" a grass island in the middle of the street.

In our minds it was like a scene from one of our favourite films A Bridge too far, I must have seen this film over 100 times. After a few hours we had finished our war and it was time for all to go home, I'm not sure if they all realise but this is one of my fondest childhood memories and will never forget it.

My best friend Wayne who sadly is no longer with us was going to join the Army; he wanted me to go with him to the careers office.

I would like to think it was because of my expertise in the area but I suspect it was because of my driving ability; Wayne could only ride a motorbike. Wayne never did join the Army but a few days later inspired from what I had heard I travelled to Birmingham careers office to follow in my father's footsteps and join The Parachute Regiment.

Wayne and I back in 1999.

I was unaware that the recruiter, who coincidentally is now a good friend, would poach me to his regiment. The opening line was "the Para's, now why would you want to do that". He then proceeded to show me a video of a challenger 2 main battle tank on ranges, I was hooked. THAT was me and I was going to be a Queen's Royal Hussar!

Having spent the best part of 14 years as a cavalry soldier in various roles a decision was made to discharge me from service along with over 100 others due to a rebranding, at this time I was on a home commitment contract in a recruiting office.

I often thought back to that day when Wayne and I first went into the careers office and it had gone full circle, it was my job to inspire others. If only Wayne would have joined, maybe things would have been different; I miss him dearly and remember it like it was yesterday.

A very proud day leading the 2017 Remembrance parade.

In 2010 I was having a few problems with my eyes, I was visiting the optician more and more, I had never worn glasses until this year and all of a sudden I had to get a new prescription every few months.

I think after about 8 visits I was referred to a specialist as they thought I had Keratoconus. Like most people I went straight onto Google to find out what this condition was all about, I was surprised to find out how rare it is.

I felt empty, why me? What does the future hold for me now? Of course I read all about the worst case scenario that I was going to go completely blind, have my driving licence taken away or even have to leave the Army. Well of course the latter happened eventually.

I see an ophthalmologist every 6 weeks, an optometrist every few months and am back and forth to the GP for medication every month. It's taken about 8 years but eventually I have come to terms with this horrible condition, it has actually helped me achieve more with my life than I could possibly dream of.

KERATO...WHAT

I am often asked what my condition is and how to spell it, sometimes even from medical professionals, the easiest way to explain it is to imagine other things that people can relate to. Imagine you are looking through frosted glass like in a bathroom, that's normal everyday life. Thankfully I have, not for much longer unfortunately the best optometrist in the country in my opinion.

Gareth has been incredible over the past few years, making sure my specialist contact lenses are the correct fit, comfortable-ish and making sure that I get the support I need. I think I must have trialed about 25 different lens types, most hurt like having grit constantly in your eye, but thankfully I have 2 lenses per eye now, one is acting like a bandage and the other to help with vision.

Vision with the lenses is ok, not perfect but good enough to drive….just.

For me being able to drive is very important, for my job, my family and for general wellbeing so for him to keep me above the threshold is amazing, I make the most of it as I'm unsure how long this will last. My condition has deteriorated over time and will continue to do so. One symptom of Keratoconus is blurred vision, in basic terms the eye is shaped like a rugby ball rather than a football and this is one of the reasons contact lenses are so hard to fit.

Most Keratoconics also suffer with what I call the kaleidoscope effect, it's a retinal migraine and in my case it makes me pretty much blind (with vision like a kaleidoscope).

Sometimes this lasts for 20 mins or other times 3 days, as you can imagine it is such an inconvenience, I have been caught out at work only once, luckily I had a nap, took my medication and it eased quite quickly, this is a reason a lot of things are not accessible for us in the employment world.

Posterior Blepharitis is another side effect that I suffer with; this is eased by medication but will never go away, my tear ducts don't lubricate, which is quite annoying when I have to wear contact lenses. Having to take them out 3-4 times a day to lubricate can be quite a nause, I also cannot wear glasses as they can't get the strength for my eyes, believe me I have tried. Certain instances I would love to throw a pair of glasses on especially first thing in the morning or last thing at night. Saying that it is probably a blessing, before my eyes were this bad I did wear glasses for a short time, I kept forgetting about them.

Making the most of every situation.

The most memorable moment was at
Borth beach, having a lovely family day
out doing what I love, climbing on rocks,
throwing stones. It's basically being a child
again and I love it.

Unfortunately a huge wave crashed against me taking my 2 week old £250 glasses into the sea, never to be found again.

Luckily my wife drives so we were able to get home, I was GUTTED, how could I be so stupid and not put my hand to my face to save them! Lesson learned... maybe!

OVERCOMING ADVERSITY

A couple of years ago I took it on myself to prove a point, to become an inspiration to show people that if I can achieve these incredible feats, anyone else can! I decided to test my eyes to the extreme, literally!

Over the years I have competed in many events including triathlon, 24hr endurance mountain bike races, 100 mile road race sportive, half marathon and a coast to coast cycle.

The one that sticks out the most is the 24hr mountain bike endurance race, the first time I was part of an Army team and we were unfortunate to miss out on a podium place, the second time I decided to go it alone and see how I got on. People with Keratoconus will know that darkness is our enemy, we struggle in low light, sunlight but mostly in the darkness and being blinded by lights, and hence why most of us don't or can't drive in the dark.

Representing the Armed Forces Para Snowsport Team, 2016.

As you can imagine riding a mountain bike on a 7 mile loop through trees, over jumps, up and down mud slides isn't too easy during the day, well imagine it at night with just a head torch or a bike light and then image it with Keratoconus, I feel it doubles the risk of falling, crashing, doing something silly.

I have crashed into trees in broad daylight so how on earth could I conquer this at night. Luckily I had a friend who started off riding in front of me, like a guide.

He soon got bored of me going so slow and went for it but it got me used to the conditions and I cracked on with it finishing 8th in my class, an achievement I wasn't very happy with at the time. I strive to be better and wanted a podium, however unlikely that was. Looking back it was a great position and one I should have embraced more than I did. I learned a lot about myself riding these events, proving to everyone that we can do these things if we put our mind to it.

I even tried out for Ninja Warrior UK but attending the casting day it soon became apparent that I wasn't going to make it, I had the balance for certain apparatus and I suppose that was from all of the skiing previously, the strength exercised however were intense. It was like I was in gladiators, the competition were all built a lot bigger than I was, and it showed on the bars, rings and pull ups.

I learned how to ski with the amazing team at Battle Back, bearing in mind I was the worse roller skater in history I was a little apprehensive with skiing, I took to it very well, skiing with a 1:1 instructor was incredible, I even conquered my fear of cable cars.

Following a week in southern Germany I was invited to try out for the Armed Forces Para Snow sport Team (formerly Combined Services Disabled Ski team). This was a huge step into the unknown for me, becoming a part time athlete, a downhill ski racer.

I must have skied more than walked that year, practically I was training non-stop with an aim to compete at the Army championships and then onto the Combined services snow sport championships, now I feel that I must say I am not disabled, I have issues but do not have a classification so could not be eligible for any formal events such as world championships and Paralympic games so the forces championships were the highest level of competition that I was able to compete in.

To me this was great, no pressure racing with a goal to complete all races entered. Within the team we have a friendly competition to all who enter, with fastest winning gold. Training saw me improve my skiing ability in many conditions with the most memorable moment of skiing fast downhill at 100kph with a blindfold on, this was to improve confidence within my guide and I, the trust between both must be unbreakable and we both had an awesome time winning the gold medal at the end of the Inter Services, with a 3rd place at the presidents race.

I am so thankful to Battle back and AFPST for all they have done for me, such fond memories.

Many sports are made more difficult by having Keratoconus, but for me it has to be a triathlon. For the past 2 years I have been part of Hereford Triathlon Club, this is a great club whether a seasoned professional or a beginner.

About 4 years ago I competed in the Leeds round of the World Triathlon Series, raising money for Bloodwise.

This was the first time the event was held in Leeds and this was all down to the success of the amazing Brownlee brothers, now I've been fans of theirs and a keen follower of the series for many years so I decided to give it a go, it was only a sprint so nothing too strenuous, or so I thought.

Training for the triathlon in beautiful Cornwall.

Swimming in dark open water with Keratoconus was tough, I had to have tinted goggles in case of glare, on this particular day it was very dull. Wearing lenses in water is not recommended but as this is competitive and I couldn't take the risk of not being able to find my bike I decided to use my lenses and push my goggles on as tight as possible. Vision was very poor, but I plodded along having to do breast stroke at times as I was so concerned about getting lost. Transition was a success and I was out on the bike having been last out of the water, I managed to overtake most of my wave and get back to where I wanted, cycling in dull light was great with my yellow lenses, pushing hard along the route felt great, I loved it. Running has never been my thing even way back when I was serving in the Army I just didn't enjoy it, but being a bit of a lunatic I gave a half marathon a go, I mean why not, we must push the boundaries to raise money for those in need.

I managed to complete the run and finish the triathlon in the middle of the wave, I was happy with my performance, and vowed to get better at the swimming so next time I could get a better result, it was then I joined Hereford Triathlon Club, they helped me improve in all aspects helping me achieve a PB in the local triathlon organised by the club.

Cycling to me was for escapism, the open road or forest, the freedom, wind in my hair, and of course being in a competitive environment, obviously this can only be a good idea if vision allows, I remember one day on a downhill course a piece of grit somehow got into my eye, now I always wear eye protection, always but it managed to get past it.

I nearly fell off hard but managed to fall into some softer grass, I immediately took it my lens out but it was in 2 halves. The pain was excruciating, I went straight to the eye department, and thankfully it was just scratched with no lasting damage although time off work as I couldn't wear lenses for a week was a pain.

Help for Heroes "Dawn Raid" 100 miles.

My most recent challenge was going to the Arctic Circle on a dog sled expedition with the backing of The Endeavour Fund, living in tents and testing my eyes at -35Degrees, a test of physical and mental strength but also testing my eye products and winning an award for my short film I made; "Keratoconus to the extreme".

The cold was so intense, water from a well would become the consistency of a slush puppy by the time it was poured into a water bottle, even going to get the water was a huge effort and energy sapping. Certainly putting my contact lenses in and out was a huge challenge in those conditions. Fingers shivering, sore eyes and frozen lens solution is not a great combination, but what an experience, another part of my life that I will never forget.

Deep in the Arctic circle with my epic dog team.

From the northern lights to a reindeer herder, relaxing afterwards at the Ice hotel to being pulled face first in the snow by my dog Rambo I have so many memories of this epic adventure, it is probably the hardest thing I have ever achieved and I'm not sure I will ever beat it, along the way I have made some truly great people, after the training and expedition these people are great friends, we all came together to get through it, ironically I now work closely with my camp mate!

Rambo, the most powerful dog I have ever met!

DRIVING ME MAD

I have always been a bit of a car geek although maybe as a child this wasn't going to be the case, at the age of 5 or 6 I had a motorbike. I remember riding it around the garden quite a lot and I also remember crashing into the fence.

Mixing Army and Motorsport, Awesome!

Quite surprisingly I have never owned a motorbike since then, it has always been cars for me.

Since passing my test 18 years ago I think I've owned 25 different cars my first one being a Vauxhall Nova. Quite sadly I had a sticker on the back saying "You've been Nova taken"! Come on, it was only a 1.2 but it did have a big bore exhaust and white viper stripes to make it go faster…

I loved my 5 series BMW though, a straight 6 engine with the sound of beauty, it only cost me £500 – oh how I wish I'd have kept it, along with a few others including the fiesta XR2i

My old beauty! I wonder if she is still running!

So my love of driving has been effected a hell of a lot with having Keratoconus, I had always just gone for a drive, see where the road takes me, many road trips and getting lost on purpose just to see if I can find my way back. This was especially a challenge when I was posted in Germany, Taking the cars on the Autobahn and driving for hours, often with a convoy of 10 cars. We even talked of setting up a local taxi company. We sometimes ended up in a glorious place, other times not so nice but that was the beauty of it.

The days of going out for a drive are quite limited these days, although I am legal to drive and do so for day to day living I can't really go out for a drive when I like, the low light, darkness, rain, or bright sun affects us Keratoconics. Thankfully I still can but it's not like it used to be, can you imagine driving and all of a sudden your contact lenses pop out or you get an ocular migraine, believe me it's not nice and one huge inconvenience especially if mines from home.

THE STRUGGLE

As I stood on a window ledge a couple of floors above the high street below me, tears streaming down my cheek wondering where it had all gone wrong. Following the previous meltdown a couple of months earlier this one seemed to affect me more, why and how had I ended up here! What is happening to me, I've always been a happy go lucky, motivated individual who wouldn't let anything stop me achieving what I wanted to.

The truth is I have no idea, I have thought about this a lot over the past few months. Could this have been bubbling up over the last few years of pushing myself to the limit or is there more to it, was it leaving the Army, so many questions unanswered and I fear I will not get this answer for quite a while if at all.

Another proud day, 2012 with HM The Queen.

This mental illness frightened me more than anything else ever has, I was doing things without realising it, making silly mistakes, becoming very lazy and it was affecting my family. I truly hope this never ever happens again, I was existing, certainly not living. A few months have passed since being diagnosed, as before I have good days and bad days but I have leveled out for the most part, I seem to struggle more when I get frustrated with things including when I have a "Bad eye day", they seem to be more regular too!

I have struggled a lot with my eyesight over the years, eyes being sore, retinal migraines, blepharitis and not being able to get the comfort with the lenses.

A corneal transplant has been talked about but for the moment I'm just able to drive, they can't guarantee after an operation such as this that it will improve my vision significantly without the use of lenses, so for me it is certainly the right decision to persevere until that dreaded moment when I lose my licence.

We often take our sight for granted and certainly I feel lucky that I am still able to do everything but having experienced blind days within my retinal migraines and corneal ulcers I appreciate my sight more than ever, we need to look after our sight. Contact lens wearers please make sure you wash hands, clean lenses regularly and do not put more than the specified amount in, recently in the press a UK surgeon found 27! Yes 27 missing contact lenses in a woman's eye. I mean that must have been uncomfortable to say the least, I can hardly bear 2, wow!

EMPLOYABILITY

A lot has been said about employment and how it is managed with Keratoconus, personally I have had what I feel as the best job in the world, The Army. Since being discharged in 2018 I tried my hand at a few jobs but just couldn't settle, I feel this was down to my eyes and not just my mental state. I would yet again have good days and bad days, for instance messing around with wires seemed like a great job, however it didn't quite work out like that, the concentration needed was immense, put that together to the amount of driving required and it's a recipe for disaster.

Always a great feeling when collecting lenses.

Having a condition such as Keratoconus isn't just the good days and bad, visiting the Optometrist and Ophthalmologist every 6 weeks causes huge inconvenience to an employer, in my case visiting Shrewsbury. This is a good couple of hours each way with most of the day spent having tests.

Most appointments also mean that I cannot drive due to the drops administered so my wife also has to take a day off work or swap shifts and the children have to be booked into after school club.

Thankfully my appointments are now not as frequent as Gareth at Shrewsbury Optometry managed to get a decent fit on my regular contact lenses, this has helped hugely in my search for a new career and thankfully I have found my dream job.

I started working for Defence Medical Welfare Service recently as a welfare officer. My role is to help the Armed Forces Community in need of help whilst in the medical pathway, to me this is not just a job, it's a way of giving something back.

I have been helped out by so many individuals and charities during my struggles and I feel it is important to repay this.

Becoming a dementia friend champion.

Many jobs that Keratoconics can't do have been talked about a lot on forums, as a qualified lifeguard I feel it would be very unprofessional if I were to be employed to save lives by "looking for danger"

The humid conditions, the fact I would have to put goggles on to jump in and the blurred vision mean that this is a definite no for any Keratoconic. The vast amount of jobs available with some TLC and sensibility means that most jobs are available.

I urge anyone to give it a go, that for me was a great way to find out if I could actually do it, be honest with employers and explain what Keratoconus is, how we struggle and what help can be put in place to make things easier and more efficient.

Welfare Officer - DMWS

REAL LIFE

My vision is currently just about good enough to drive, some are not as lucky as I, it's very much an individual case by case, I certainly can and having being a car enthusiast for as long as I can remember is a huge bonus, I am not quite sure how I would feel if I couldn't drive although I do have some idea as some days I can't even get my lenses in meaning I can't function, it's hard enough doing anything never mind driving. To me it's all about being honest and not to do anything silly, it's just not worth it, if I feel I will struggle then I simply will not drive.

Invictus training, swimming every day!

During the early days with Keratoconus I didn't do much sport at all, I found it a hard thing to do, swimming in particular was a sport I wanted to do again, as a child I loved swimming and wasn't too bad at it either.

I have been a qualified lifeguard and was even part of the regimental swimming team when based in Germany. Most people will advise not to wear contact lenses in the pool and for good reason, but imagine going swimming without being able to see where you are going, most people who wear glasses will know what I mean, and most will wear glasses in the pool or get prescription goggles, many times I have stubbed my toe, got into the wrong pool, fell in and even walked into the lifeguard station so I decided to see what I could do with goggles and contact lenses, certainly anything is possible with Keratoconus but you just need to take more care, don't wear lenses in the water, or if you have to then use a very good suction pair, I have found a pair made by Vorgee (Terminators) and they are amazing, they even have a darkened lens for the brightness for outdoor swimming or artificial light

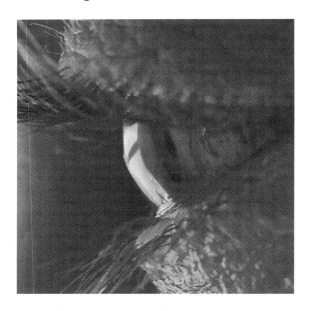

My cone shaped cornea.

I often get asked what annoys me the most about Keratoconus, I have a list as long as my arm but for me it's having to take my lenses out and clean them, some days its once and others it seems like 20 times, it's really annoying if you are out and about, especially on the tube in London. A trivial one is getting out of bed and having to sort lenses and eyes out before you can do anything, it would be lovely to just be able to see first thing, this is a very common thing with us Keratoconics.

I often find it difficult to get lenses back in, especially in very humid weather, cold weather and of course if I am outside, my advice would be to
try and take time and don't rush things, make sure you have everything that you need and have clean hands.
If you are like me you will get very frustrated if your lenses are uncomfortable and in the early days I used to get very angry at myself, especially if I needed them for work. I now take 3 spare sets (Soft as a bandage with RGP on top), spare drops and medication everywhere I go.

I make everyone aware of the condition so they can hopefully understand if I need to take time out, or move from certain light. When I was first diagnosed I kept it to myself as I didn't want to feel different, my understanding was that they wouldn't want to employ me as I was too much of an inconvenience but thankfully most people are very pleased that you confide in them and they do what they can to help. I now embrace it and it is who I am.

I like to think of myself as a Keratoconus Ambassador and will continue to try and do my best, inspiring others who are being diagnosed and not knowing what is next.

My "Spares" are carried with me wherever I go!

WHERE NEXT?

Help is available through any optician,

hospital, online groups and the most

important way I feel is speaking out, if you

are struggling then just ask.

A great starting point is an online help forum, Keratoconus GB ran by Rae, since being diagnosed Rae has helped me in more ways than she knows and I will be forever grateful, She single handedly runs the webpage, forum and many requests. I would like to say this platform was a great way of meeting likeminded individuals, gaining knowledge of what the condition is like and I now feel that I am able to help others thrive rather than just survive.

Thank you for taking the time to read about Keratoconus and me, I really do hope I have been able to show what can be done if you put your mind to it, even with a condition such as Keratoconus!

My lifelong ambition is to climb to the top of the world, Mt. Everest, then again whose isn't…

ACKNOWLEDGEMENTS

I have so many people to thank, first and foremost my family, whom I have dedicated this book for, without them I don't know what life would be like. Gareth Hardcastle in my eyes is the single best optometrist in the country, I will be forever grateful for everything. Mark Scorgie, Jen Kehoe, Bob Case and AFPST who helped me achieve something I never thought possible and to believe in myself. Ian O'Grady and the Endeavour Fund/Fortitude team, that Arctic expedition was incredible!

I must also mention the National Keratoconus Foundation, a US based foundation, one that has also helped me in the past. Giving me the desire and belief to enter two short films into their film festival competitions, I was so humbled to become a runner up in year 1 with my adventure exploits and the winner in year 2 with my arctic expedition film.

Finally to Lofty who allowed me the time to do all of these adventures.

Huge thanks to those who have helped and supported me, as you can imagine I have so many people to thank, the list would be as long as this book! So to everyone at The Queen's Royal Hussars, Help for Heroes, Invictus Foundation, Fight for Sight, The NHS, Hereford Triathlon Club, SSAFA, RBL, KeratoconusGB, DMWS.

Ski racing with AFPST – amazing times!

IG17 UK Team trials @Bath Uni.

Printed in Poland
by Amazon Fulfillment
Poland Sp. z o.o., Wrocław